ST. LAWRENCE SEAWAY

A TRUE BOOK

by
Ann Armbruster

Children's Press®
A Division of Grolier Publishing
New York London Hong Kong Sydney
Danbury, Connecticut

Reading Consultant
Linda Cornwell
Learning Resource Consultant
Indiana Department of
Education

Subject Consultant
William D. Ellis
Editor of the quarterly journal
of the Great Lakes
Historical Society

A pilot boat in the
Soo Canal

Library of Congress Cataloging-in-Publication Data

Armbruster, Ann.
    St. Lawrence Seaway / by Ann Armbruster.
        p.   cm.   — (A true book)
    Includes index.
    Summary: Tells the story of the construction of the inland waterway
which links the midsection of North America to the world.
    ISBN 0-516-20016-X (lib. bdg.)   ISBN 0-516-26114-2 (pbk.)
    1. Saint Lawrence Seaway—Juvenile literature. [1. Saint Lawrence
Seaway.] I. Title. II. Series.
F1050.A75 1996
971.4—dc20   96-2086
                                                              CIP
                                                              AC

Contents

Thanks to the St. Lawrence Seaway, ships can travel all the way from Lake Superior to the Atlantic Ocean.

4

Canada and the United States

Canada and the United States are countries in North America. They are friendly neighbors with common borders.

They also share three coastlines. The Atlantic Ocean stretches along the east coast of the North American continent. The Pacific Ocean

5

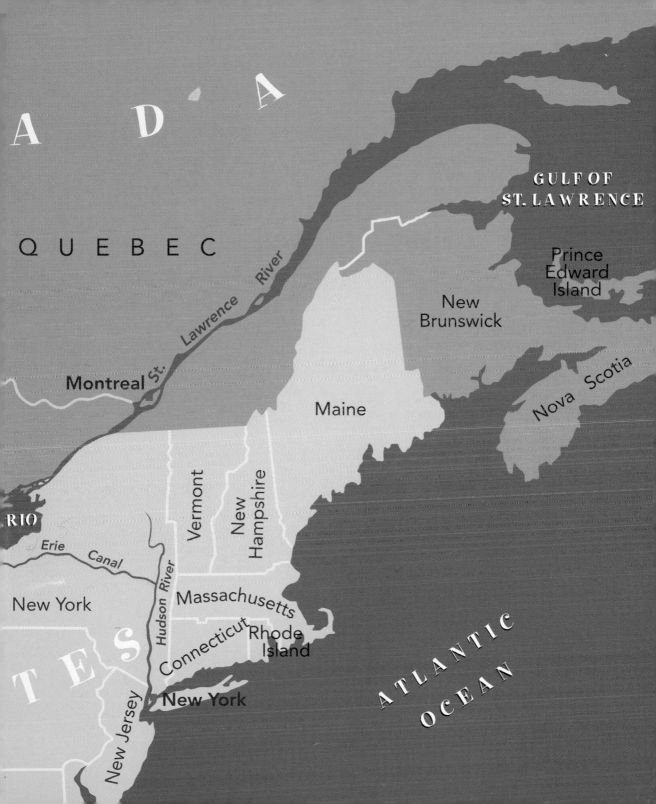

borders the west coast. The St. Lawrence River and five lakes between the United States and Canada are often called the "third coast."

Lake Erie, Lake Huron, Lake Michigan, Lake Ontario, and Lake Superior make up this group of lakes. They are known as the Great Lakes, the largest group of freshwater lakes in the world. The St. Lawrence Seaway, an international water-way, links the Great Lakes to the Atlantic Ocean.

Explorers and American Indians

In 1535, Jacques Cartier, a French explorer, crossed the Atlantic Ocean. He was searching for a water route to China and Japan. Instead, Cartier found the St. Lawrence River. It is the second-longest river in Canada. Only the Mackenzie River is longer.

Jacques Cartier (left) sailed the St. Lawrence River. He then founded the first French settlement in North America.

The St. Lawrence River flows almost 800 miles (1,300 kilometers) from Lake Ontario to the Gulf of St. Lawrence.

In the 1500s, the Algonquin and Iroquois Indians lived in the heavy forests along the riverbanks. Many animals, such as beavers, wolves, and bears, lived in the forests, too. The Indians often traded

Algonquins building a lodge

animal furs with the explorers in exchange for steel axes, mirrors, and bright cloth.

The American Indians called the 2,342-mile (3,769-km) route from Lake Superior to the Atlantic Ocean the "river without end." Later, the waterway would be an important link between the Midwest and the Atlantic Ocean.

During the 1600s and 1700s, many European explorers and settlers arrived in

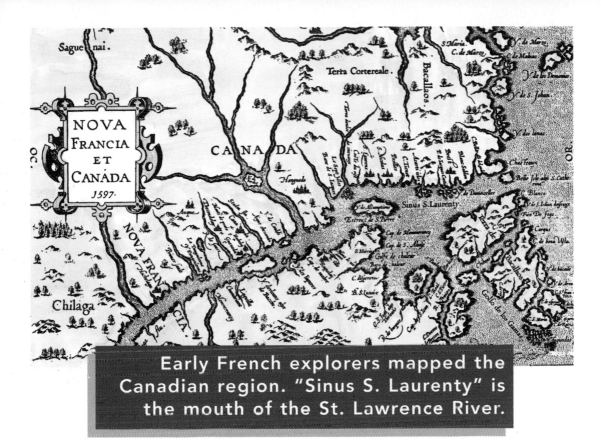

Early French explorers mapped the Canadian region. "Sinus S. Laurenty" is the mouth of the St. Lawrence River.

North America. The Indians taught the Europeans the ways of the wilderness. Swift birchbark canoes carried the newcomers on explorations and trade routes. In winter

A canoe travels through dangerous rapids (above). The Indians taught the French how to use snowshoes (right).

months, Indian snowshoes helped them walk over deep snow. The explorers followed Indian trails. Some of the trails became the modern highways of today.

Transportation

Travel by water was dangerous. Sudden storms often hit the Great Lakes. Strong currents and high waves could bring sudden death. Some early business leaders and contractors built ditches or canals to bypass the rapids on the St. Lawrence River.

The Great Lakes are known for their storms (left). Travelers on the St. Lawrence River had to steer their rafts through rapids (right).

Boats and supplies had to be carried around Niagara Falls.

By the mid-1800s, sailing boats and steamships traveled on the waterways. They carried cargoes of fur, grain, and lumber. An increasing number of immigrants arrived from Europe, drawn by the promise of low-cost land and jobs in lumber camps. Rich iron ore deposits were discovered in Michigan and Wisconsin.

Immigrants from Ireland poured into the region during the mid-1800s.

Canals and Locks

Canals were built to improve travel on the waterways. The United States built the Erie Canal in 1825. In 1829, the Canadians completed the Welland Ship Canal. This canal links Lake Erie and Lake Ontario, allowing large ships to sail around the steep and

To avoid the Niagara Falls, ships use the Welland Ship Canal.

powerful Niagara Falls. The canal was enlarged twice to fit larger ships.

The Erie

The building of the Erie Canal was an important feat in the history of the United States. Once completed, *it connected Lake Erie to the Hudson River in New York.* The canal helped New York City become a leading port during the 1800s.

Canal

The first boat through the canal was the *Seneca Chief*. It carried Governor De Witt Clinton of New York and other officials. When it arrived in New York Bay on November 4, 1825, fireworks lit up the sky. The governor poured a keg of Lake Erie water into the bay to symbolize the union of the Great Lakes and New York.

The water level of the five Great Lakes varies, falling from Lake Superior to the St. Lawrence River. Ships that pass from one lake to another may need to be raised or lowered to the next water level. Locks were installed in the canals to serve as "elevators" for the ships.

Locks are like huge boxes built into the ground. They are open at the top. Each lock has gates that keep water in or out. To raise a

These locks on the Erie Canal at Lockport, New York, raise and lower ships to new water levels. Here, the water is being drained from a lock as a ship makes the trip down.

ship, a lock is filled with water so the ship floats up. To lower a ship, the lock is drained.

Later, the Soo Canals were built at Sault Ste. Marie, on the border between Michigan

and Ontario, Canada. One canal is located in Canada, and the other two are in the United States. The Soo Canals connect Lake Superior and Lake Huron.

The St. Lawrence River became a major trade route when the canals were completed.

Construction Plans

By 1895, Canada and the United States discussed plans to deepen the canals and the St. Lawrence River. The joint project would create a system of locks and canals to connect the lakes with the Atlantic Ocean. It included a hydroelectric power station. It would also open the river for large ocean ships.

Before the St. Lawrence Seaway, railroads carried goods to the Atlantic Ocean (left). Coal is an importance resource to the Great Lakes region (right).

At first, industries in both countries were against the project. Railroads and ports on the Atlantic Ocean claimed this route to the sea would take away some of their freight business. Coal companies feared power stations would reduce the amount of coal burned for electricity in the seaway area and cut their profits.

In both countries, however, groups of people also worked for approval of the seaway. After fifty years of debate, the two nations reached an

In March 1941, the United States and Canada signed the St. Lawrence Seaway agreement. Here, J. Pierpont Moffat, the United States minister to Canada, signs his name.

agreement. Each country would be responsible for improvements within its own waters. A system of tolls was established with both nations sharing the income. Work on the seaway began in 1954.

The construction of the St. Lawrence Seaway was a tremendous engineering job. The Jacques Cartier Bridge at Montreal, Canada, was raised 80 feet (24 meters) to provide enough room for tall ships.

Workers clear a channel for the Dwight D. Eisenhower Lock (left). Many rocks (below) were moved during the seaway construction.

Workers dug a channel 1 mile (1.6 km) long through a bed of hard sandstone. At some points they had to drill and blast through 2 miles (3.2 km) of solid rock.

The construction of the
St. Lawrence Power Dam

Both Canada and the United States built dams to use the power of the St. Lawrence River. These hydroelectric dams would provide electricity for homes and industries in New York, Pennsylvania, Vermont, and Ontario.

At last, the canals, dams, locks, and bridges were complete. Highways and railways were relocated, and entire communities were resettled. The incredible job was finished.

Finding a New Home

The project was not good news for everyone. During the construction of the hydroelectric plant, a man-made lake 30 miles (50 km) long was created. It wiped out seven towns. About 6,500 people had to move their homes and businesses.

In this photo, we see people walking alongside their houses, which are being dragged over the ice to new locations. Some movers put a glass of water on the kitchen table to show the owners that they could move the house smoothly, without spilling any water!

The St. Lawrence Seaway

The St. Lawrence Seaway opened on April 25, 1959. Two months later, U.S. president Dwight D. Eisenhower and Queen Elizabeth II of Great Britain dedicated the seaway. The royal yacht, *Britannia*, crossed through the

When the seaway was complete, President Eisenhower and Queen Elizabeth II helped celebrate (above). Finally, ships could sail easily from lake to lake (left).

ceremonial gates to make the opening official.

It had taken five years to complete the seaway. Finally

there was a complete water-way from the westernmost lake—Lake Superior—to the Atlantic Ocean. More than 360 million tons (330 million metric tons) of rock were dug up in the process. The seaway includes 65 miles (105 km) of canals, 15 locks, and 3 dams. And all the canals are at least 80 feet (24 m) wide and 27 feet (8 m) deep.

The seaway is open from early April to mid-December.

Early Canadians dig up the ice from the St. Lawrence River (below). Ice on the Great Lakes makes it difficult for ships to pass (right).

During the winter months, ice clogs the St. Lawrence River and ports on the Great Lakes. The cargo is there, but the ships can't reach it.

Geography

The St. Lawrence Seaway lies in the United States and Canada. It links the midsection of North America to the world. The Great Lakes and St. Lawrence region covers an area of almost 1.5 million square miles (3.8 million square km). There are more than 50 ports within this region.

The ports of Duluth, Minnesota (above), and Quebec City in Montreal harbor (right)

The Canadian provinces of Quebec and Ontario lie along the northern border. The Great Lakes states of New York, Pennsylvania, Ohio, Indiana, Illinois, Michigan, Wisconsin, and Minnesota are located on the southern border.

Industry

The St. Lawrence Seaway is now one of the world's great trade routes. Cities located far from the Atlantic Ocean, such as Montreal, Cleveland, Toronto, Chicago, and Duluth, are now ocean ports. Grain from midwestern farms and automobiles from Detroit, Michigan, can be shipped overseas via the seaway, rather than

Industries grew with the opening of the seaway, such as agriculture (above) and iron mining (right).

sent by rail to eastern ports. Iron ore mined in Quebec can be transported to other countries. In one year, more than 200 million tons (180 million metric tons) of cargo moved through the U.S. Sault Ste. Marie locks.

Industry and trade grew within this region. Mining and forest

The steel (left) and timber industry (above) also flourished.

industries appeared. The manufacture of steel, appliances, cars, and machinery increased. Major shipyards sprang up to produce military ships and 1,000-foot (305-m) supercarriers. A giant industrial and agricultural area was born.

Benefits

Both Canada and the United States benefit from the rich economic region formed by the St. Lawrence Seaway. In good weather, large ocean vessels can travel the 2,342 miles (3,769 km) of the seaway in eight days. Locks raise ships as high as 60-story buildings as they pass through the

Large freighter ships travel the St. Lawrence Seaway, bringing the wealth of the Great Lakes to the world.

waterway. Industries can move products in and out of North America at a reasonable cost.

The building of the St. Lawrence Seaway is a story of cooperation between two countries. It is one of the greatest peacetime accomplishments in history.

To Find Out More

Here are more places where you can explore the St. Lawrence Seaway and the states and provinces around it:

 **Books**

 **Organizations**

Gelman, Amy. **New York.** Lerner Publications, 1992.

MacKay, Kathryn. **Ontario.** Children's Press, 1992.

Nirgiotis, Nicholas. **Erie Canal: Gateway to the West.** Franklin Watts, 1993.

Provencher, Jean. **Quebec.** Children's Press, 1993.

Sherrow, Victoria. **The Iroquois Indians.** Chelsea House Publishers, 1992.

Great Lakes Commission
400 Fourth St.
ARGUS II Bldg.
Ann Arbor, MI 48103-4816
(313) 665-9135
glc@glc.org

New York State Department of Economic Development
Division of Tourism
1 Commerce Plaza
Albany, NY 12245
1-800-CALL-NYS

Information Tourisme Quebec
Case Postale 20 000
Quebec City, Quebec
Canada G1K 7X2
1-800-363-7777

 **Online Sites**

Explore Quebec
*http://www.iisys.com/
quebec/quebec.htm*

At this online site, you'll
find useful information
about Quebec and environ-
mental projects along the
St. Lawrence Seaway.

Discover Montreal
*http://www.cam.org/
⋯fishon1/montrea.html*

Find out more about
Montreal's history, attractions,
architecture, and tourism.

Visit New York
*http://www.roundthebend.
com/*

Here's New York State, right
at your fingertips. The state is
divided into sections. Pick the
one you want, and explore!

Facts and figures about
the Great Lakes
*http://www.great-lakes.
net:2200/refdesk/almanac/
almanac.html*

Includes information about
populations and the region.

Visit Ontario, Canada
*http://www.great-lakes.
net:2200/partners/GLC/pub
/circle/ontario.html*

On Ontario's Great Lakes and
St. Lawrence River shores, you
can visit parks and see base-
ball, museums, and wildlife.
Tour Toronto, Hamilton,
Niagara Falls, and more.

The New York Seaway
Trail
*http://www.great-lakes.
net:2200/partners/GLC/pub
/circle/newyork.html*

Travel the New York Seaway
Trail, a 454-mile (730-km)
route along Lake Erie, the
Niagara River, Lake Ontario,
and the St. Lawrence Seaway.

Niagara-on-the-Lake
*http://www.niagara.com/
chamber.notl/*

Niagara-on-the-Lake is just
a few miles from the
famous falls, with a history
and attractions all its own.

Important Words

canal man-made waterway for boats

cargo goods that a ship carries from one place to another

current fastest part of a body of water

freight business of carrying goods

hydroelectric dam barrier built across a body of water that uses water power to create electricity

immigrant person who travels to a new country to make a home

ore mineral that holds a valuable substance

toll place where one must pay money in order to pass through

yacht type of boat used for racing

Index

Meet the Author

Living in Ohio, close to the Great Lakes, Ann Armbruster pursues her interest in history. A former English teacher and school librarian, she is the author of many books for children.